THE REAL PURPOSE BEHIND THE HAT

"The Broken" Leading "The Broken"

TERESA A. STITH

THE REAL PURPOSE BEHIND THE HAT

Copyright © 2018 Teresa A. Stith

All rights reserved. This book is protected by the copyright laws of the United States of America. This book may not be copied or reprinted for commercial gain or profit. The use of short quotations or occasional page copying for personal or group study is permitted and encouraged. Permission will be granted upon request.

Unless otherwise identified, scripture quotations are from the King James version of the Bible. Copyright © 1982 by Thomas Nelson, Inc. Used by permission. All rights reserved.

Please note that certain pronouns referring to the Father, Son, and Holy Spirit may be capitalized to acknowledge God and any such titles referring to Him. Please note just the opposite when referring to satan. We choose not to capitalize his name or acknowledge him in any way, even to the point of violating grammatical rules.

ISBN-13: 978-0692111505
ISBN-10: 0692111506
Publisher- A Faith That Works Publishing
Website: afaiththatworks.com

THE REAL PURPOSE BEHIND THE HAT
"The Broken" Leading "The Broken"

When it's so much easier to die, BUT PURPOSE commands you to LIVE!!!

"I declare" says God, "the end from the beginning and from ancient times things not yet done. I declare how things turn out long before they ever happen. I declare not just natural events but human events- doings, things that are not yet done."

Stop acting like you don't know
what it means for **ME** to be
GOD (1)

-John Piper

DEDICATION

This book is first dedicated to God for giving me the ability through grace to discover and walk in my purpose. I struggled for years trying to discover what my purpose truly was, and even after finding out, dragged my feet to walk in it. There is something about operating in purpose that we sometimes do not readily accept. We often find ourselves questioning whether or not we are equipped to perform or carry out the thing that we have been called to. Remember this, that who the Lord called, He also qualified. The Bible tells us in Romans 8:30 "Moreover whom he did predestinate, them he also called: and whom he called, them he also justified: and whom he justified, them he also glorified." My hopes are that you may be free to identify and expose your own inner battles that you too may be free to walk in the thing wherewith you have been called. For it is not by might, nor by power, but by My Spirit saith the Lord of hosts (Zechariah 4:6).

There are so many inner workings and hidden secrets and thoughts that battle us on a daily basis that makes it hard for us to believe and accept that we have been called and chosen to lead others. We must know that we serve a God who is no respecter of persons and who has already liberated us, tried us through our afflictions, and set us up for this very season of our lives.

To my Leaders who rooted and grounded me in the faith. For blessing me and instilling in me the courage, the boldness and the strength to fight on despite the odds that were against me. They made me realize that there was still so much more worth fighting for. For inspiring me to believe and trust in God's timing. They said "For the vision is yet for an appointed time, but at the end it shall speak, and not lie: though it tarry, wait for it; because it will surely come, it will not tarry" (Habakkuk 2:3).

To my family who are witnesses both of my struggles physically and my transformation spiritually to a new life in Christ Jesus. I'm thankful for my oldest son Marqui who has been my greatest critic, always reading my work and critiquing me on my grammar and other things. Thank you son for not only reading my work, but taking the time to breath in those parts that ministered, spoke volumes to you, and caused you to face your own issues in life. I tell you what peace you will have when you finally learn to apply these principles to your life and believe God for greater, BUT GOD is working it!!!

    To my brothers and sisters in the faith who have prayed with me and walked with me through the trenches when I was just about on my last leg. Those who were there for me in the wee hours of the morning or late at night when I just needed an encouraging word from the Lord or a good shaking up to get me going again. Those who have challenged me to do my best work with praise on my lips and joy in my heart, when I wanted to throw up my hands and quit.

    And to my best friend Sue, my twin in the gospel, I just cannot put into words the sacrifices that you have made for me. The covering you have provided for me and the spiritual shield that God has given you to protect my Spirit. Thank you for just coming by sometimes to grab my hands and pray and declare victory in the name of Jesus. My powerhouse in the faith. Whatever God has blessed you with, you've never refrained from sharing it with me. A true Sister indeed. I could never repay you for your generosity. Get ready my Sister to reap what you have sown!

    And to you, the men and women all over the world whether you hold a leadership position or not, through blood, sweat, and tears, have worn more than just one hat. In doing so, you have brought about change, hope, and inspiration to those on the verge of maybe taking their own lives. You have given them a purpose and a reason to live. You are a special kind of people and not everyone is equipped to do what you have done. You may never get that pat on the back that you feel like you deserve, but know that your service to others have not gone unnoticed. God declares that He is not unjust; He will not forget your work and the love you have shown Him as you have helped His people and continue to help them

(Hebrews 6:10, NIV).

      For what is a leader? A leader is more than just someone who bears the title of "leader." A leader is someone who positively models the way for others. He or she is someone whose leadership has been so effective that it has caused a complete change in the lives and in the behavior of others for the better. Being transitioned into a position of leadership is a reward truly worthy of its honor and recognition. It is an accomplishment that not only showcases and highlights the individual's talents, gifts, and abilities but his or her deep love and compassion for what they do and those for whom they do it. A leader is one who shows commitment, empathy, honesty, and integrity. Someone who is able to make good decisions and have good communication skills. This character or charisma will potentially draw others and build on them a long lasting impression suitable to be passed along for generations to come. You were stretched, ridiculed, rejected, separated, set aside, disrespected, shamed, and even BROKEN…but through all of that you were equipped with patience, honesty, integrity, a genuine heart for change, trustworthiness, support, and the ability to lead by example. You were put into a leadership position because you are strong enough to handle it. You have something that has been birthed inside of you called PURPOSE, and whatever your role has been up to this point, you were molded *for such a time as this.*

I TIP MY HAT TO YOU ALL.

TABLE OF CONTENTS

Chapter 1: Getting to Know Your Purpose..........1

Chapter 2: Accepting Your Purpose……………..13

Chapter 3: All About God…………………………41

Chapter 4: The Healing Environment………………….51

Called and Qualified…………………………………….63

Chew on This……………………………………………...67

About The Author……………………………………...69

Bibliography……………………………………………….71

WHAT IS THE STORY BEHIND YOUR HAT?

PREFACE
You Are What You Eat, Or Are You?

We may not have the power to CHOOSE the life that we would like to live, but we can certainly contribute to how well things play out by paying attention, being obedient, and putting into practice the things that we have learned that are beneficial to our overall health and growth. The Bible says "Beloved, I wish above all things that thou mayest prosper and be in health, even as thy soul prospereth" (3 John 1:2).

We all have our own opinions as to what "the best" life consists of. Whether we have acquired this knowledge through research, observation, or personal experience, no one can change the course of our lives but us. How we choose to live life will determine its success or failure. I certainly agree that it is easy for one to become a product of his or her own environment, but I also agree that not everyone does. My own life is a testament of this statement. At a time when it looked as if young girls were only having babies and going on welfare (governmental assistance), I knew that I wanted better for my life. I did not just sit around and *think* that I wanted better, I started *taking the steps that were necessary* to *get to* that better place. It was certainly not going to fall out of the sky! If you have run this race and could have easily fallen into the pitfalls of your environment, but didn't, then ask yourself…why not?

    See, my will to live and survive what I was going through ultimately became greater than the will to give up. I said *"ultimately became"* because I did not start out in this great "wanting to survive" mode. I had to get there, and let me tell you, it was not easy. I battled depression, suicidal thoughts, isolation, rejection, feelings of worthlessness, feeling unloved, and a host of other emotions prior to arriving at this place of "freedom" in Christ.

There are those of us who are weak minded and will go with whatever the wind blows our way and there are others who (although they may be weak minded too at times) based on this social environment, still manage to remain strong enough to choose to overcome the struggle and rise above the chaos. Which one are you?

I remember going to lunch in the third grade and as I was eating, I looked up and there was a banner plastered across the dining hall wall that read: "You Are What You Eat." I will never forget how I felt as I continued to eat my lunch wondering if I would turn into some of those beans or that hot dog that I was chunking down. As a child, I was not sure what would happen, but I kept eating (laugh out loud).

I never forgot these words as I maneuvered through life for it was this very phrase that taught me that I will always have the upper hand at choosing what I wanted to (eat) do with my life. It most certainly taught me to be careful how I prepared my meals (life situations). Now, I have not always made the best choices in the foods that I have eaten, for I have eaten things that have had me running off for years (smile), but it was this seed that was embedded in me so many years ago that has now sprung up into a life filled with substance and order, joy, and unlimited possibilities. I will tell you that I have even gained a few pounds (chosen foods or situations that were not so good for me) over the years, but I'm grateful to know that I have options (making wise decisions, dieting) available to me to get the weight off! But…we all have that choice. Choose wisely.

Writing this book has given me great joy as I wanted to acknowledge and encourage every leader and those who aspire to become leaders to continue to be your unique selves. We are often met with challenges beyond our ability to endure, but we keep pressing forward despite our obstacles. Sometimes it seems that the higher we go up the ladder, the more evil we are subjected to and must endure, but we do so with patience and joy knowing that those coming after us will not only benefit but continue the race with grace, dignity, and respect for all individuals. Always remember that with such a wide variety of foods available, you don't have to eat the same things over and over, you do have the freedom and the will power to switch things up a bit. I'm reminded of this old gospel hymn that states:

> Come over here where the table is spread
> and the feast of the Lord is going on.

God will prepare a table for us, in the presence of our enemies, but we have got to make sure that we are in our rightful places and connected to the right people to receive all that He wants to give us in this season.

Get ready, Get ready, Get ready for the overflow!

I press on to reach the end of the race

and receive the heavenly prize for which God,

through Christ Jesus, is calling us.

-New Living Translation

I run toward the goal, so I can win the prize

of being called to heaven.

This is the prize God offers

because of what Christ Jesus has done.

-Contemporary English Version

I keep pursuing the goal

to win the prize of God's heavenly call

in the Messiah Jesus.

-International Standard Version

But now thus saith the Lord that created thee, O Jacob, and he that formed thee, O Israel, Fear not: for I have redeemed thee, I have called thee by thy name; thou art mine

Isaiah 43:1

INTRODUCTION

In "The Real Purpose Behind The Hat" Teresa shares her experiences with you in finding her own purpose for living. We have all asked the questions "Why am I here?" "What is my purpose in life?" "What did God call me to do?" and "Why was I even born?" I tell you, I was so caught up in a whirlwind of emotions and thought that my life was so tragic, that I began to pay attention to the things that were happening in hopes of finding clarity amongst the chaos. I thought that it could not be humanly possible for any one person to experience all that I was going through, and still maintain their sanity. I began to watch other people lives to see if they were going through anything like I was.

It was at this moment that I realized that I was looking for a crutch. I needed someone to lean on.

Someone to not make this all just go away, but someone who could make these birth pains a little less severe! When you have purpose being birthed inside of you, it doesn't just go away. The pains of this birth can be worse than giving birth to a baby, and what mother has ever smiled through that portion of the birthing process? It's certainly not impossible, it's also not normal!

    The way to discovering your purpose can seem like a long road leading to nowhere fast. I found myself trying to model my life after other people, the problem was that nothing from their lives seemed to fit into mine. We cannot live anyone else's life, only the one that we have been given, so never desire to walk in someone else's shoes. I became envious and jealous at times to see other people lives blossoming and mine appearing to be one big rollercoaster ride. I was going through the same things over and over and over again. I could not seem to get the victory over anything! God continued to remind me of Psalms 37 to not be envious of those who seemed to prosper in their ways.

There were times that I questioned my faith because I lacked the understanding as to how "this thing" (my faith and my life) was supposed to work. What I discovered, as will many of you, was that I was already walking in my purpose! Because it was not what I thought it would be or because it did not look like what I thought it should, I did not recognize it when it came.

What will your purpose look like when you stumble upon it? You may never know, but I encourage you to keep walking, keep doing what it is that you do and do not be surprised if like me, you walk straight into your purpose without ever realizing that you have arrived.

What is the thing that you are most passionate about? When I looked at myself, I could not seem to figure it out at first. I mean it took years for me to realize what my gift/purpose was. I love to sing, and I love music. I love every instrument that comes together to make the sound of music. I thought that singing would have been my platform to a better life and although I still sing from time to time, I realize that singing is a gift, but it is not my purpose. I tell you, I use to swear by God that He had not given me a purpose. I could not sew or knit, decorate, design, or do any of the things that many of my friends and family seemed to excel in. I struggled trying to find a job so my skill set was very low. But I absolutely loved to read, write, and go to school. I loved English, grammar, spelling, and anything associated with teaching. There was something about learning that I just had a passion for. I loved to teach and instruct. I remember how miserable I was when school was closing for the summer. I would solicit the teachers to give me the extra paperwork that they had at the end of the school year and I would use them to play school at home with my brothers and sisters, and guess who the teacher was? Yes, me (laugh out loud)! It is amazing *what things* God will put in us even at birth, but then…life happens, and amidst the chaos and the noise of our circumstances, we forget all about *that thing* and we find ourselves searching for it (purpose) all over again.

  When I became employed at a correctional facility, I was grateful for the opportunity to be able to minister to those in prison. For more than 20 years, I would like to think that I have inspired, and given hope to many that I have come in contact with. I have watched offenders lives change right before my eyes. Some have even left the system and gone on to become productive members of society again. I have learned much from them as well as they from me, for they have not known my brokenness while fighting to endure various stages of my life. Some of their stories have inspired me to continue to contend for the faith that has been delivered to the saints (Jude 3).

Live your life as you discover your purpose and pay attention as you may already be doing the thing that you have been chosen, inspired, and equipped to do. Do it with love, do it with perseverance, and do it with PURPOSE. For you have been chosen to do this.

You are capable of making the biggest transformation of your life. Significant, lasting changes shouldn't take you years. But it means stepping beyond your current way of life and embracing new habits. To create the level of life you ultimately want, you have to change something you do daily. Your life is your signature creation. It is your duty to live true to yourself, with authenticity. Your life's mission is to express yourself boldly, create what you love and love what you create. It's about expanding and living your vision of yourself---- until it is the greatest possible expression of who you are. (2)

-Thomas Oppong

And the Lord God called unto Adam,
and said unto him, Where art thou?
And he said, I heard thy voice in the
garden, and I was afraid,
because I was naked; and I hid myself.
And he said,
Who told thee that thou wast naked?

CHAPTER 1

Getting To Know Your Purpose

For years I have asked myself "what is my purpose for living?" "Why am I here?" "What does God want me to do?" I've gotten a lot of opinions about what I should be doing from others, but still not any real closure or peace about it, so I sought the Lord for the answers. Although there were periods in my life where I felt like I was being punished, I understand now that I was actually being molded. Everything that I put my hands to that failed was teaching me patience and how to seek God more in depth for what I desired. It also taught me how to pray and ask for things according to God's will for my life. I had my first child when I was seventeen years old and still being a child myself, struggled with how to provide for another human life so I went on welfare. The struggle was real. I could not seem to find meaning and purpose in life so I became suicidal and depressed. I was broken mentally, physically, and spiritually, but this brokenness was my key to discovering who I really was. I got so fed up with situations (that I ultimately had no control over) but began to realize that these things are not going to change unless I do something to change them. I tell you the truth, things got pretty ugly and very messy, but at least I was no longer stagnant. I was taking the steps that I needed to take to fix my life.

    One thing that we have got to be ready to do is be willing to get down and dirty with our own selves. We cannot be afraid to challenge ourselves in the process of discovering who we are and what we were called to do. We have to be brave enough to tell our own selves no! For what is your flesh but your own sinful nature? It only does what we allow it to. It is as powerful as we give it the power to become.

I would like to think that I have not been alone in the search for purpose. Many of us have sought after it for much of our young and adult lives and some of us are still not sure what it is. I tell you what, it bothered me so much at one point that I questioned if I even had a real relationship with God. As I mentioned earlier, I did not have any job-related skills growing up because much of my life was lived basically trying to survive as best I knew how. I remember myself and my siblings going next door to our neighbors house, sometimes to borrow money and other times just to eat. My life was one struggle after the next. I was a very emotional person growing up and I took things to heart so easily. Everything affected me. What people said, what they did, their actions, attitudes, etc. I never expressed my feelings about these things, but I kept them bottled up inside. When I was alone, I would ponder on those things and try to understand or make sense out of them. I was very observant, but I could also discern a lot about people. I think this is what led me to keep myself distant from others. I was a loner. There were times that I sought to make myself fit, but those temporary moments of relief did not last long.

Although my life was chaotic, it was rather interesting to me. Everything was a lesson. The only problem was that it took years to understand that these lessons were meant to serve a purpose, to teach me something, to grow me. All I needed to do was to pay attention, but I was so distracted. My God, there

The Real Purpose Behind The Hat

was always something else that seemed to draw me away from the things that I should have been doing that was truly necessary to move me forward. And guess what? The longer it took for me to see it, the longer it took for me to come out of the mess. I'm talking about Y-E-A-R-S!!! For years, I was so focused on me, me, me…what I wanted, what I didn't want, who I wanted, who I didn't want, what I wanted to do, what I did not want to do…just a total mess. I was mentally drained in the struggle to figure out what was actually going on, I felt like I was caught up in a whirlwind. I was only two steps from being committed to a mental health ward. I had to decide to slow down my mind, control all of these thoughts that were bombarding me continuously and get some order and control over my thinking. Not an easy thing to do, but possible!

Teresa A. Stith

    I used to ask people all the time, "what's my purpose?" and whatever they said, I accepted… hmmph, *I didn't know*. It amazes me how desperate we can become sometimes that we are willing to accept anything that someone else says without any second thought. I just wanted to feel validated. I wanted to feel like I was included, and that I belonged in the moves that God was making that became so evident in the lives of other people.

    Knowing what your purpose is will be a uniquely different experience for every individual because no two people will walk into their destinies alike. For some, the road will be easy, for others it will be rather difficult and challenging. This depends on a lot of things, but namely OBEDIENCE! If you are anything like I was…hardheaded, disobedient, stubborn, mean, and unteachable, you will suffer.

The Real Purpose Behind The Hat

Suffering did not mean that I was being punished, however, I was being chastised (corrected). The Bible tells us in Proverbs 3:12 "For whom the Lord loveth He correcteth; even as a father the son in whom he delighteth." Because God delighteth in me, He sought to teach me His ways. His rod of correction bruised me, and He became pleased with what He had wrought in me.

> Yet it pleased the Lord to bruise him; he hath put him to grief: when thou shalt make his soul an offering for sin, he shall see his seed, he shall prolong his days, and the pleasure of the Lord shall prosper in his hand.
>
> Isaiah 53:10

In getting to know your purpose, be mindful that setbacks are bound to happen and will be a part of your experience. Do not be discouraged, it is all a part of your process. Do not allow not knowing your purpose to cause stress and bitterness toward those who seem to be walking in theirs. We don't know someone else's story. What you may be seeing on the outside is nothing compared to what that person may have had to suffer internally. Let's get excited about how we see God at work in someone else's life and remember, you may already be doing the thing that God has called you to.

    When I stopped worrying God about what my purpose was and continued to live my life, is when I discovered that I was already busy doing what I was called to do. I had to laugh at myself because I was looking for some big off the wall thing to happen. In Isaiah 55: 8-9, we learn that "God's thoughts are not our thoughts, neither are our ways His ways," declares the Lord. God works in the most simple, yet amazing ways and we often miss His hand at work because we are looking for some "out of this world" thing to happen. He is nearer to us than when we first believed! Relax, and rest in the Lord. When your time comes you will walk into your purpose. You won't have to question it or second guess it. The only thing that you will be able to proclaim is…thank God I have arrived!!!

When Love Takes You In

When God's love takes us in, it takes us in for good! There is NOTHING that can separate us from the love of God (Romans 8:28). Looking at Romans chapter 11 and how God grafted the branches back in again truly blessed my soul. It helped me to see that even when we error in our ways or reject God as sometimes we do, God does not rain fire from Heaven or dismiss us, but He incorporates it into His ultimate plan for our lives and our salvation. He knows what is needed to save us. God knows how each of us will find Him. His plan for how I found Him will be different from the one that may be needed for you to find Him. We all will have that "something that drove us to Christ" experience unless you choose not to come to repentance, you do have that choice. But it just amazes me how every pain that I felt through rejection, depression, fear, etc. was a setup for me to call on the name of Jesus and experience the love, joy, peace, and comfort that God provided and gave me access to through Jesus Christ.

When loves takes you in, you go from death to life. I tell you what, when someone leaves this world people will flock to a funeral for whatever reason. Some sincerely want to pay their respect to the deceased, others want to see the reaction of those grieving, and then there are others who just go to see who else went. Whatever the case may be, thank God for the good that even comes through death. Sometimes people reconcile and settle differences, they forgive and forget. Death draws people together if only for a moment especially if it is someone well-known or popular in the community. Some are left to consider their own ways as death is a wake- up call for them to get their houses (bodies, life) in order. I said all of this to say that when love takes you in, you do not have to fear death, hell, or the grave. DIE!!! In getting to know your purpose, choose to DIE. Die to your flesh, die to your own will, die to fear. Perfect love casteth out fear, for there is no fear in love (1 John 4:18). God will never let you fail. That's a promise that you can rest in.

Teresa A. Stith

Are You Ready To Die?

I once thought these things were valuable,

but now I consider them worthless

because of what Christ has done

(Phillipians 3:7).

-New Living Translation

But what things were gain to me, those I

counted loss for Christ (Phillipians 3:7).

-King James Version

CHAPTER 2

Accepting Your Purpose

One thing that I have learned while discovering my purpose is that I had to be willing to wait for God to reveal my purpose to me. In the process of waiting, I became anxious, impatient, and frustrated with God because He was not answering me as quickly as I thought He should. Well, God not answering was not the problem at all, He had indeed answered me, but I was so busy looking for something else, that I missed Him completely. I could not hear God speaking to my heart because there were so many other things that came in the form of distractions, that I allowed to block my thinking and blind my mind. It is safe for me to say that I understand why God does not reveal certain things to us before its time because if He did, some of us could not handle it. We would go off and start doing our own thing and veer off the path that God has ordained for us to travel. Some of us would become so full of ourselves that God would not be able to do anything with us.

If anyone had told me that my purpose was to go inside a prison and preach the gospel to convicted felons for 20 or more years, I would have told them that they were crazy and to do it themselves (laugh out loud). But here I am more than 20 years later, still sharing a word with whomever chooses to listen and accept a word that can change the course of their lives forever. If anyone had said that I would write books about my personal experiences that would motivate and encourage others, I would not had believed it. But here I am, a Published Author and Owner of my very own Publishing Company "A Faith That Works Publishing." Stepping into your purpose before your time can be dangerous and ineffective. It could leave you in a dry place with all kinds of emotional attachments. Let me tell you about my journey….

I can recall sitting in my church this particular day in a meeting that my First Lady (my Pastor's wife) was having with the Women's Group at my church. I was telling her about my job at the correctional facility where I was employed as a Food Operations Manager A. The position was coming to a close and I was subjected to becoming unemployed unless I wanted to lateral transfer into another position, which was that of a Correctional Officer. Of course I did not want to do it and I expressed this to my First Lady who said "Teresa, God said "don't make Him have to put a bit and bridle in your mouth like they do the horses when they want them to go a certain way." I knew in essence that she was saying that this is the way that God wants you to go, don't fight it, just trust God through it!

Being a Correctional Officer meant more exposure to the offenders, their living quarters, and more interaction with them in which I tried to avoid at all costs. I wanted to avoid them because at one point in my life, men was a problem (weakness) for me. It wasn't that I did not trust the system, I did not trust myself around them…BUT GOD! All we would hear at that time was another female who had fallen into the clutches of some offender and was walked off the job (fired) for fraternizing. You will never know that you have been delivered from a thing, if that

The Real Purpose Behind The Hat

thing never comes back to try you. Not only that, I knew that the female officers were made to wear their shirts inside their pants and I definitely did not want to do that. See, I was still scarred, and in the process of still healing from some other very traumatic issues with men. I did not want these men making any derogatory remarks or expletives toward me in that regard at all. I am saved and I wanted to be respected and seen this way. Let me interject here and say this: when God has a purpose and a calling on your life, the devil knows about it too. Do you think that he is going to stop his rampage against you and treat you any differently because of FAVOR? No!!! The devil already knows clearly what God's plans are for your life before you do. His mission is to stop that plan from existing so he gathers together all his little imps in the hopes of wreaking so much havoc in your life that you will throw up your hands and quit. Yeah, I wanted the men to respect the "Christ in me" but guess what they did? The complete opposite (laugh out loud). God will not let everything that you experience be peachy. Something has to come to try those areas in you that have not been completely healed yet. Those things that we would like to conceal and not reveal. Although we do a very good job of hiding these things from people, they cannot be hidden from God and He knows how to get them out of us. Those offenders called me everything but a child of God at times, and guess what I did? I cursed them right back!!! As a leader and as a child of God, I had to be taught how to conduct myself in the face of adversity. I learned that it was not always having to strike back with a closed fist or with some vulgar language. I was still a little rough around the edges. I

The Real Purpose Behind The Hat

had to be disciplined. But God dealt with me. He taught me. The Lord said to me one day "how do you expect them to respect you when you're acting just like them?" He said, "you cannot even hold them accountable because you are just as wrong as they are." This is what caused me to change, but I had to be willing to not only look at it, but accept the part that I was playing in contributing to the chaos around me. God was challenging me to be renewed by the transforming of my own mind, so that I could actually help those still in bondage to this way of thinking and behaving. I learned to maintain my professionalism! After that day that the Lord spoke this to me, when the offenders came cursing and carrying on, I would say to them, "sir I am not cursing you, can you please not use vulgar language?" some of them apologized and refrained from using it but not everyone did. Those who did not, I held accountable, but of course I had to be consistent with my behavior as well. This is what ultimately brought about changes in the offenders. I had to model the behavior that I was expecting from them. When you understand that it's not about you and it's all about God, you can walk it out. But either I could accept this new position or become unemployed. I had 4 young men at home who were dependent upon me to provide for them so, I could not afford to be anywhere without a job. I accepted the position.

I was scared to death! Prior to accepting this position, I had so many issues with men through failed and abusive relationships, lust of the flesh, etc. I had developed a severe hate in my heart toward men. I dealt with them on my job because I had to, not

The Real Purpose Behind The Hat

because I wanted to. I had developed the attitude that men get what they deserve, and I did not feel sorry for them. I felt that their only motive in life was to seek out some poor, lonely woman and take advantage of her by lying to her, cheating, and getting out of her whatever seemed to be beneficial to him. Men disgusted me. I began to rejoice in their downfalls and sufferings. In my mind, I was healing myself so I felt justified. Hmph…all they put me through. Good enough for them. I was so bitter and cold toward men. I know that this all sounds so mean and harsh, but I have to be real about where I was. If I don't tell you the truth about where I was, you will miss the glory in God bringing me out of that place. I developed these false perceptions of men all because of one or two bad experiences. I had no compassion for them at all. I laugh as I recall some of my male friends telling me that I was so inapproachable. They said that I carried around this look that said "keep walking and do not say anything to me" so they did not speak to me! On the flip side, I was at home praying and asking God "what is on me, that is causing people to dislike me?" "God why?" I said, "am I not being noticed by men?" I laugh now, but it really hurts my heart to know that I was so deeply scarred that I could not see the affect or strain that my anger and bitterness toward men was having on my relationships with those around me. BUT…I kept being chosen to lead!

Although I had been put into a leadership position, I had a hard time trusting those under my supervision. I felt like everyone had some ulterior motive. All that I had ever known was people telling me that they would do this or that, and making promises to me but never keeping their word. People were deceitful, but I had my guards up. I may had looked tough on the outside, but my heart was tender and pure, I was only protecting my heart. My love for people was so great and I loved them so deeply that when they hurt me, it was a pain that only one who loves like this can understand. I stopped allowing myself to get close to people and I kept it professional with them. Nobody seemed to be able to hear my screams for help, but they were so loud to me that I did what I was accustomed to doing to drown out the noise…I put up a wall. I was void of understanding, so I suffered quietly.

One night one of my officers (Officer Boyce) came to me and asked me "why don't you trust us to do our jobs?" I'm sitting behind my desk shocked that she even approached me like this, but admiring her for "challenging the process". I explained to her that it wasn't that I did not trust them, but as a supervisor, I am still ultimately accountable whether they did their jobs or not. I told her that she had to understand my position. I explained to her that when I come to check her post, I'm not saying that I don't trust you to do your job, but part of my job is to sign your paperwork and ensure that certain things *are being* done. That seemed to be an easy enough explanation right? Wrong. Of course when Boyce left my office, I pondered on that thing a little deeper and I asked God to show me how to be a better Manager and not just a stern or strict Supervisor. There is a difference. I did not want people *to not* want to work for me, so in my brokenness, I still had to listen and be led. But I could not lead effectively, if I was not hearing correctly. But God was surely with me. We

The Real Purpose Behind The Hat

need to stop thinking that because someone is not on our level physically, that we do not have to receive instructions from them or listen to them. We all know how God used an ass in the bible to speak to Balaam. If you don't know, you can read it here (Numbers 22).

I'm also reminded of a day that I was walking in downtown Lawrenceville, Virginia at the time, and I saw one of my brothers, John. I was so glad to see my brother because I loved my brother and I knew that whatever I asked him for he would give it to me, if he could. So I rolled up on my brother this particular day like I'd done many times in the past, with my hand already out looking for him to give me some money. My brother chewed me up and spued me out (laugh out loud)!! I had never been so humiliated in my life! I asked my brother for some money and my brother told me to get a job! He told me to stop laying up somewhere having babies and could not provide for them. When my brother was finished with me, I wished that I had never saw him that day!!! I mean he literally just tore my day all the way up. It was like someone had stabbed me in my heart. I was angry with him for a long time after that but failed to see the truth in what he was saying because of what I wanted from him at the time. I remember saying "who is he to say this to me, to check me?" He said "god lee, how many kids you gon have?" I mean he put so much emphasis on how he said it that I felt nasty just hearing it from him. But I tell you what, it made me start looking at my own self. I felt ashamed, but this shame bought so much conviction that it ultimately caused the change that I needed to clean up my life. I began to make better decisions for my life. I told God on my brother, yes I did. I said "Lord he ain't even saved, tryna tell me something." But God dealt with me! I was the one professing to be saved, so why did my brother who did not know Christ at the time, have to put me in my place? See when God is trying to get your attention, He will dry up those worldly resources that we keep running back and forth to. And He will put a word in an unsaved man's mouth to give to you! I couldn't see Jesus because I was always looking for my brother to provide for me. Until God shut it down! He knows how to turn your focus back on Him! God said "no, he may not be saved, but he is telling you the truth."

As leaders, we have to be willing to accept what other people see about us. As long as people are dancing around and patty-caking with you, and not telling you the truth, you are being hindered from not putting forth your best effort and moving forward.

Sometimes we are blind and ignorant to our own ways and God may allow others to expose these things so that we can look at them. We must be willing to accept that we may be the change that we want to see in others. When we choose to change and correct the error of our own ways, we will see the change in those that we may have prayed for or still believing God to change. Change begins with each individual admitting first that change is necessary. When this happens, everyone wins and we all can rejoice, rather than you gloating or glorying in your own selfishness and false ambitions.

    There was a man on my job, Cpt. Rowe. I owe him so much and pray for the day that I can see him again to hug his neck, embrace him, and tell him thank you. I weep now as I recall his compassion toward me. He saw me in my brokenness, and he

The Real Purpose Behind The Hat

ministered to me in ways that I will never forget. He does not know that he played such an intricate role in my restoration in Christ during this time. I will forever speak of his goodness to me while under his supervision. Cpt. Rowe called me into his office one night and he pleaded with me to tell him what was going on. I was silent. I had been displaying some very strange behavior that was not consistent with my job performance at the time and he became aware of it and confronted me on it. He stated that he had been instructed to write me up because I had missed so much time from work. I was so depressed during this time that I would pull into the parking lot for work and decide that I did not want to be there, and turn around and go back home. I would not call or go in to work. I would go back home and cry and deal with my issues as best I knew how. He said "Mosely" (my name at the time) "what is it?" "What can I do to help you?" "whatever it is" he said, "we can get through it together." I just sit there in his office and cried. He said "Mosely, I don't want to write you up, but you have got to work with me here, give me something that I can work with." Let me make this clear. My decisions to not go in to work during this time were not done because I thought that I could do it and get away with it. I was battling depression. Depression is a serious deep rooted issue and if not treated or handled properly can lead to suicide or death. My will to live was buried underneath the chaos, the circumstances, and the brokenness that I was experiencing. I was literally watching my life fall apart. There were so many broken pieces, that I did not have the strength to even begin to sort out and put back in order. I just wanted to die and escape it

The Real Purpose Behind The Hat

all. People have died because they feel that their problems are greater than their ability to overcome them. Lieutenant Earl Hawkins saw me come in to work one day and he called me to where he was and asked me "what is wrong with you?" He told me that he had never seen me look like this the whole time that he had been knowing me. He told me that I looked a hot mess, my hair was a mess, and that he did not want to see me looking like that ever again! I had never been more humiliated! This crushed me. Lt. Hawkins was known to crack jokes every now and again, but it was something about his stance, his facial expression, and body language that told me that it was nothing funny about what he was saying, and that he meant what he said. These were people that I KNEW cared about me as a person, but I did not feel that they could handle me spiritually so I did not confide in them spiritually. I fought the battle alone. Isn't it amazing how God will send someone to speak a word, even reproof to you and it does more for you than what you are able to see with your physical eyes? Every time someone stopped me and inquired about what was going on, although it hurt me and made me cry even more, God was making me look at my situation, and it was freeing me. It was easy to go home and lay down in my mess, but when I begin to look at it, the power to overcome it seemed attainable. So I started fighting to win the battle. Thank God for Jesus! BUT, after a few more call-ins, Cpt. Rowe was left with no choice but to refer me for disciplinary action to Alphonso Hicks, my Colonel at the time. He along with Major Tracy Jarrell went through the same scenario trying to get me to understand the importance of coming to work and following the

The Real Purpose Behind The Hat

policies that were in place that I was clearly in violation of…BUT…they didn't understand where I was and I did not want to talk to them about it. This was clearly not a departmental issue that I was dealing with, but because it affected my work performance on the job, I was disciplined accordingly. I left his office with a Group I offense on my record, but I still had a job, so I was thankful.

Not too many days after that as I was preparing for work and ironing my clothes, I began to feel really good. I mean just out of nowhere, it appeared to be this black blanket that I see being lifted off of me. I mean I can literally see it in the Spirit floating up off of me and I felt good. I went in to work and everyone is looking at me like "what in the world happened to her?!!!" Everyone was so amazed, people were telling me how good I looked, how I was glowing, etc. They asked me what happened, I said "I just feel really good today." I told them that I was ironing my clothes for work and it appeared to be this black blanket lifting off of me. I will tell you that today I understand that I was under a spiritual attack from the enemy, BUT GOD had already prepared the way for me. He had the right people in the right places and the right positions that He allowed to show me mercy and compassion in my time of need. I am forever grateful to these leaders who have inspired me over the years. If God has never used you before, He certainly used you here. I'm truly grateful for that.

Even in all of this, I would like to think that God already knew my innermost feelings toward men and against them when He sent me to work in this prison. See, we can't say that we love God (whom we have not seen) if we cannot love our brothers or sisters whom we see every day (1 John 4:20). So I came to realize that when we say that we love God, God will put us in situations to test that love. And what better place to put me to test my love for Him, but in a place where I felt like I hated everyone! My God…My God!

Now we know that if God call us to do something, then He has already equipped us for the task at hand. I did not know that I was equipped, so I went in emotions first! I was already angry and upset because I did not want to be here in this environment with all of these men. I felt that they were all scam artists and just trying to smooth talk their way through everything just like the guys on the street, so I didn't believe a word that any of them said ever! Because I love the Lord, I had to eventually go to God and ask Him to show me how to communicate with these offenders, afterall, I did not want to disappoint God if He sent me here for a purpose. I asked for forgiveness in how I conducted myself while bearing the Lord's name and I set out to do better.

Once I broke the ice and decided that I would communicate with these offenders, I learned things about them and about my job. I began to think that maybe they were not all bad people, but people who made really bad choices in life. As I began to listen and let down my judgmental guards against them, I was able to effectively minister the Word of God, motivate, encourage, and help these offenders have hope. I learned that they had already been given their sentences by the courts and that I had no right to further punish or accuse them of anything. As God began to show me His love, and I began to release my own brokenness to Him, I began to experience freedom in my life. Those parts that still wanted to be bitter, broken, and justified, God replaced with His grace and His love. The more I ministered the Word of God, the more freedom I began to experience. This part of my journey reminds me of Jonah in the bible and how Jonah got upset and frustrated with God because he wanted God to destroy the city of Ninevah. I wanted God to destroy some men. I was blaming every man for an issue that I had within myself that I refused to deal with. Isn't that just like some of us? We always want God to deal with other people, but we refuse to take responsibility for our own actions which may have been the root cause of someone else's response toward us. I tell you, Ninevah, avoided the wrath of God when they repented (Jonah 4: 5-11). We too, like that great city of Ninevah, will have to repent for wanting God's vengeance to fall on others, when we have been just as guilty in some things. As I released my heart to God, He showed me how to love and accept people for who they are, suspending all judgment because He's the Only Righteous Judge.

In accepting God's purpose for your life, let God cleanse you thoroughly from yourself that you are able to submit yourself totally to Him as you boldly proclaim "Lord thy will be done." You will never be able to accept God's purpose for your life clinging on to dead stuff. God will send you into places that your flesh may not want to go, but know that God is with you through it all. Who would have ever thought that after being mistreated by men my whole life, that God would put me in a place to

The Real Purpose Behind The Hat

minister to them? Oh, but God!!! The word says in Romans 11:33- 34, O' the depth of the riches both of the wisdom and knowledge of God! How unsearchable are his judgments, and His ways past finding out! For who hath known the mind of the Lord? Or who hath been His counsellor?

It is all about God! Yield yourself completely to be used by God in any way that He sees fit. Learn to accept His purposes for your life and do not be fooled into thinking that you are safe because you've created a path of your own. We can run, but we certainly cannot hide from the plans that God has already ordained for us. No matter how long it takes, YOU WILL do the thing that God has said. Jonah, and other prophets in the bible ran and hid themselves from God instead of doing what God instructed them to do. In the end, God got the glory out of their lives and those that they were sent to minister to were saved from destruction. Don't let God have to chase you down, submit yourselves under His mighty authority that He may exalt you in due time (1 Peter 5:6).

> Commit thy works unto the Lord, and thy thoughts (plans) shall be established (Proverbs 16:3)

> Commit thy way unto the Lord, trust also in Him; And He shall bring it to pass (Psalms 37:5)

CHAPTER 3

All About God

As much as we would like to make this about us, it is not about us, it is ALL ABOUT GOD! If we think that we are living this life to become rich and famous or to make a name for ourselves, we are sadly mistaken. Maybe we have thought that we would build large bank accounts and live free from financial strain and stress while enjoying the finer things in life, well these are all our own twisted ideas. God has no interest in the plans that we have made for ourselves for he says plainly in Jeremiah 29:11 "For I know the thoughts that I think toward you" saith the Lord, "thoughts of peace, and not evil, to give you an expected end." This is not to say that God does not want us to work and enjoy nice things, it's when we lose focus of Him that our journey becomes one of insignificance. If we can bear in our minds that it's all about God, then God will be the motivation behind every decision that we make and all of the plans that we develop. As noisy as things can become, when we quiet our own Spirit to know what God is saying, we will not be led astray.

I was having a conversation with one of my sons, and my son Lord knows, wants to do God's will but he is often distracted by things around him. It could be people or some thing that has come to challenge him, but he gets all bent out of shape at the first sign of a test. He's fine as long as he's not being tested. He will read the word, tell you what he think it means, but when it comes time to apply it to a situation or circumstance, he loses focus. He's so blinded by the test, that he can't see Jesus! I had to take him all the way back to Matthew chapter 14 where the disciples encounter Jesus walking on the water. They were afraid and cried out in fear, but Jesus told them not to fear because it was indeed Him. Peter, of course says "if it be thou, bid me come unto thee on the water." And Jesus responded, "Come." Peter walked upon the water like Jesus did, but became so overcome with the winds and waves around him that he lost focus of Christ and began to sink. Aren't we like this? We do well on our journeys as long as we are not being tried and tested. The moment something arises to challenge us, or our faith, or the way that we have become accustomed to doing certain things, we become defensive. We have become people who do not like to be told what to do. We do not like instructions. We feel that we already have it going on and anyone who challenges what we think we know, becomes a threat to us. Oh stop it! The bible says in Romans 10: 17 "So then faith cometh by hearing, and hearing by the word of God." We have got to be willing to listen and learn regardless of what we may think that we know. The Lord revealed to me at one point that I was unteachable. To hear God say this to me was unbearable. It broke my heart. Why would God say this to me? What did He mean? Rather than argue with God about what He meant, or why this was said, I searched the scriptures and my own heart for understanding. I pulled out the dictionary, the bible, I prayed, etc. I truly wanted to know what God was seeing in me that I was obviously blinded by. God showed me plainly that I did not listen, that I spend an awful lot of time trying to know everything. When people would come to give me instruction, I quickly cast it aside saying "my way is better." What I found was that people did not want to work with me. Not only that, I was working myself to death. Why? Because I was afraid to let others in. I was afraid to let down my guards and trust others in this process.

Now I will tell you that I am a learning fanatic. I love to learn. I am always looking to learn and gain a new perspective on things. I love to read. We must be careful what we allow into our Spirits while reading. If I'm reading something and even if I believe what I'm reading, if the word of God tells me something differently about the thing, I need to believe the word over what I read. This is why I had become so unteachable because I had read so much and had become so convinced about what I had read that when God tried to show me the truth about a thing, I did not want to receive it because of what I had read. My, My, My…I'm so thankful that God goes to such great lengths to ensure that we have understanding for "the Lord is not slack concerning His promise, as some men count slackness; but is longsuffering to us- ward, not willing that any should perish, but that all should come to repentance" (2 Peter 3:9). I thank God that even in our ignorance, He stands ready to forgive and help us along the way. My son is learning now how to hear God. He is realizing that even at our best, we still need God. When we put God first and include Him in our business, He will lead us and guide us like never before. When we began to make God our trust through every issue of life, our ears will become more sensitive to His voice and we will know when He is speaking. Our eyes will be opened and we will began to see how God is working, we will began to understand His ways and learn how He moves. We will become so connected to God that we can feel His breath upon us, breathing life into every place our feet treads. He will began to give us favor and others will look at us and wonder and even ask "Who is this God you serve?" When it is all about God and not about us, the depth of the riches of the glory of God is made known unto us and we began to have GOOD SUCCESS!!!

God Prunes and Grafts

To prune means to cut back dead branches and weak parts so that they can thrive and grow better.
Or it could mean
to weed out unwanted and unnecessary things.

Teresa A. Stith

A graft is a young branch or a twig that has been placed into a slit on the trunk of a living plant to receive sap from it.

Grafts may die from a lack of water.

Grafts are also pieces of tissue that is transplanted surgically.

Now, when it is all about God, God begins to cut off and weed stuff out of our lives whether it is people or things. The important thing to remember is that as God does the separation of these things, we should not go back and reattach ourselves to them. We should be drinking plenty of water (living water) and eating (the Word of God) which sustains us and gives us life. Our nourishment does not come from any other source but God. We cannot grow fully

The Real Purpose Behind The Hat

if we do not go through this process of separation. The bible tells us in 2 Timothy 2:4, "No soldier in active service entangles himself in the affairs of everyday life, so that he may please the one who enlisted him as a soldier (New American Standard Bible). We are not called to be people pleasers, but simply God pleasers. God has chosen us and enlisted us in this battle. He will not let us lose. We bless God when we honor Him with what He has given us. It is not for us to gain, but for Him to get the glory. When God gets the glory, then He will in turn reward us openly for our faithfulness to Him.

> O the depth of the riches both of the
> wisdom and knowledge of God!
> How unsearchable are His judgments,
> and His ways past finding out!
> (Romans 11:33)

Teresa A. Stith

For you formed my inward parts;

You knitted me together in my mother's womb.

I will praise you, for I am fearfully

and wonderfully made;

Marvelous are Your works;

my soul knows it very well.

My frame was not hidden from you,

when I was made in secret, intricately woven

in the depths of the earth

(Psalms 139: 13-15).

Chapter 4

The Healing Environment

The Department of Corrections has developed an initiative called "The Healing Environment", it's meaning is described below:

The Healing Environment is PURPOSEFULLY CREATED by the way we work together and treat each other, encouraging ALL to USE THEIR INITIATIVE to make positive PROGRESSIVE CHANGES to improve lives. It is safe, respectful, and ethical- where people are both supported and challenged to be accountable for their actions. (3)

As you can see, some parts of the initiative were bolded to give a deeper impact or perspective on how each of us can contribute and control our environments. Even though this is an initiative developed by the Department of Corrections, I would like to share some spiritual insight into it.

Purposefully Created

We were all purposefully created to be used by God. When we understand our purpose, what we do with it and what we do in it will have an overwhelming impact on those we were chosen to lead. God created you on purpose so rejoice! The bible tells us that many are called, but only a few are chosen You were selected by God Himself to LEAD. How effective you are in leading others will determine to what extent you were HEALED! You cannot lead others while you are bound. What I experienced during this time was that I was beginning to attract other people to me who were also broken and bound. So here we are, all sitting around using one another as a crutch and drowning in our sorrows. To lead others, somebody has to be free! You have got to be able to see where you are going.

> Let them alone:
> they be blind leaders of the blind.
> And if the blind lead the blind,
> both shall fall into the ditch
> (Matthew 15:14)

When others' vision is blurry, *WE* should be able to stand boldly and profess that "there is hope for the hopeless." We should be able to tell them that "you will make it, you will survive." "Dry bones CAN live!!" If you are in an environment that looks defeated, you have the power to command freedom by how you see it, how you react to it, and what you are speaking in it. You were purposefully created to command your environment to be healed!

I'm reminded of a story in the bible from Numbers 13 when Moses sent men to spy out the land of Canaan. The men came back with a negative report that although the land flowed with milk and honey, there were giants in the land and that they looked like grasshoppers compared to those who dwelled there. But Caleb silenced the people in front of Moses and said "Let us go up and take the land at once, for we are *well able* to overcome it!" You must have faith in the power and the promises of God so that you can boldly declare what thus says the Lord. Unbelief will make you overlook or forget what God has said about your environment and the power that you possess to change it. Dare to be different, dare to trust God regardless of how things look. Sometimes faith will let you stand alone, but when you do…trust that there are more with you than those who may be against you. Ask God like Elisha did, "Lord I pray thee, open his eyes, that he may see. And the Lord opened the eyes of the young man; and he saw: and, behold the mountain was full of horses and chariots of fire round about Elisha" (2 Kings 6:17). Dare to step, dare to speak, dare to command, and let God do the rest.

Use Your Initiative

We each have that special something that we bring to the table that is so uniquely different from what anyone else may bring. We are our own unique selves. We can all use our initiative to bring healing, restoration, and life to our environments. Now, *your environment* can be your own individual self for *this place* is wherever you need healing. Sometimes we have to deal with ourselves before we can deal with other people. If you can speak life to yourself, then you can certainly speak life to your surroundings. If you do not have the power to speak life to yourself then it may be a bad day for everyone else, especially if you are the one leading. BUT there is hope, because there may be someone in your environment that has more power than you do, so they can ultimately command peace to follow you. Are you all hearing me? This does not mean that the person with the power is after your position or seeks to have any authority over you, it simply means that we should know those who has been assigned to us and know where we can go to get the help that we need to endure. If you and everyone else in your environment is negative, you will have one bad day after the next.

The Real Purpose Behind The Hat

Nothing will ever work right until you decide that you need help, not be afraid to ask for help, and know exactly where to go to get help. The bible says that pride goeth before destruction, and a haughty spirit before a fall (Proverbs 16:18). This means that if you are too conceited or self-important, something will always come to make you look like a fool.

    I was fortunate enough to sit amongst a very elite group of people one morning as we discussed how we as individuals could change or contribute to our environments, whether at home, on the job, in the community, etc. by choosing to surround ourselves with the right kind of people. That even if we are surrounded with people who are not like us, we can still use our initiative to change the way that they think. I was rather disappointed though, in some of the negativity that was brewing in the meeting and the fact that it was coming from someone who was "seasoned" in this environment. I tell you the truth, no matter how much time and effort you put into building something, it only takes one negative person to come along and try to destroy what you built with their "set in their ways" opinions. And let them tell it, they are right in what they say and will not let anyone tell them differently. I think I said it earlier, they have become "unteachable". They cannot see pass their own views to see things any other way except their way. An environment cannot be healed if there are people in it who refuse to embrace change and see things from another perspective. Some of the things that were said bothered me because to heal an environment, people have got to be willing to take responsibility for their own actions. I'm hearing other people from the President, to politics, to those in

The Real Purpose Behind The Hat

leadership positions being blamed for the corruption, and mishaps that tends to occur in an environment that is unstable or unproductive. Leaders were even blamed for failing to engage with those on the lower levels. And not that any of this wasn't true, but my question was and still is "how can YOU contribute to the environment?" See, because things may not change in the hierarchy like we think that they should or as soon as we feel that they should, but your environment still has to function. What are you doing to see that it does? We cannot wait for things to change at the higher levels, we have to be committed to do what we can from where we are and we have to be able to inspire others to do the same. When everyone in your environment share the same goals and vision, things will began to change and everyone is rewarded. Use your initiative to bring inspiration and hope to those dependent upon you to lead. Stay connected to your life source that you may be able to empower those who may not see the vision at first. Be patient in the process and overcome each obstacle and challenge with grace and perseverance.

Progressive Changes

Change will not happen overnight! It did not take one night for the environment to crumble and it will certainly take more than a day to rebuild. Everything that contributed to its demise, must be brought into account and challenged so that your environment will not falter again. How is this done? You have to go in and tear down some things! You have to know what works well for your environment and who works well in your environment and make the necessary adjustments. In changing the course of my own environment (my life) I had to be willing to change the way that I was looking at things. I became very frustrated because I wanted to see changes right away. I felt that I was wasting time going through a lot of drama that could have been avoided. So why wasn't it avoided? Because it was challenging something in me that I did not want to look at. I did not want to change, it was too costly to my flesh. I wanted to be in control and do my own thing. When God began to strip me of my will, and made me humble myself and submit, I thought I would die. Technically, I was dying. I was dying to always having my way and I began to yield to the Spirit of God in me. Again, everyone's experience may not be the same, but it is important for you to know what you need and then be willing to seek help from the right Source. For my sheep hear my voice, and I know them, and they follow me.

Teresa A. Stith

Have you been looking at your purpose all wrong?

Have you missed the clues along the way?

The biggest barrier to discovering your

purpose isn't that you're screwed up

or broken;

it's that you've been looking at

it in a disempowering way (4)

-Mike Lamele

IT'S ALL ABOUT GOD!

The Real Purpose Behind The Hat

Called and Qualified

We may not know this, but God does not call the qualified, He qualifies the called! You may have asked yourself, "why would God choose me?" Just know that if you have been chosen, be obedient to the call. Luke 9:62 tells us that "No man having put his hand to the plough and looking back is fit for the Kingdom of God." Don't run away from what God has designed to be a blessing to your life.

There are certain qualities that God looks for in us for He knows what He has put in each of us. He expects us to be faithful, committed, well-beloved, walking in truth, giving and spreading love, and honoring Him with what He has entrusted into our care. Our souls must prosper, and it does so when God's character is revealed in us. Faith worketh by love and our love for the Father is shown through our faithfulness to Him. God's love qualifies us to be IN THIS PLACE! You cannot work for God in a ministry if LOVE is not the driving force behind what you do. Understand what you are doing and the motive behind it for this is where God's favor comes from. Don't become so accustomed to struggling that you miss the simplicity that comes from trusting God and taking Him at His word. For years I struggled with myself and my ability to perform what God often said that He had equipped me to do. I could not fathom in my own mind that God had counted me worthy to do such things. When I looked at my own life, I often felt that I shouldn't be telling anyone anything. I'm so grateful that God moved me pass this stage in my life

The Real Purpose Behind The Hat

and taught me to appreciate the new wine that He was able to pour into me through obedience, faith, and trust in Him and His spoken word.

> Not that we are competent in ourselves to claim anything for ourselves, but our competence comes from God (2 Corinthians 3:5)

God's best for us comes through obedience to Him. God can call us and He can even qualify us for the work that He has chosen, but we still have to CHOSE to obey the call. Remember, do not allow fear to keep you from the thing that God has purposed for your life. Stop trying to figure God out and learn how to trust in His plans. He knows what He is doing.

Teresa A. Stith

Seize Every Opportunity

to make a difference in

the lives of others.

When you're walking

in purpose,

Favor goes before you

and your steps are

ordered

The Real Purpose Behind The Hat

Chew On This

It is not meant for everyone to go with you as you go forth to do what God has called you to do. I will share with you that this journey has been one of complete excitement, joy, and at times a little overwhelming to say the least. It has been overwhelming with the respect that this is a road that I have never traveled. To see God put things together, even to the point of connecting me to the right sources and resources has been nothing short of amazing! While I am enjoying living life on PURPOSE, this place has also been one of rejection, fear, and uncertainty. Those that I thought I would have had the most support from, I've had the least. I have been afraid at times to go forward and trust my own heart. When you discover your purpose KNOW

THIS, God will not leave you alone! The thing that I have learned to do is STEP IN FAITH! The bible tells us in Hebrews 11:6 that without faith, it is impossible to please God, for he who comes to God must believe that He exists and rewards those who diligently seeks Him.

Do not refrain from living out your purpose because you are waiting for others to get on board. You may have to walk alone. You have to get to a place on your journey where your eyes are fixed (on Jesus) and your mind is made up. You cannot allow yourself to become so entangled with the affairs of this life that it hinders your answer to the call. If God is the driving force behind what you are doing, then do it with all diligence so that you can please the ONE who called you to do this. Remember, it is all about God, that He might get the glory out of our lives.

The Real Purpose Behind The Hat

About The Author

This is the second book written by Teresa, the first being the popular "A Faith That Works, Moving From Seeing To Believing." Her upcoming titles include "Live Like You Know, Embracing Our Freedom in Christ," "Writing About Writing, What Every First Time Writer Should Know," "A Faith That Works

Teresa A. Stith

Devotional For Men," "A Faith That Works Devotional For Women," and lastly "Advancing The Kingdom of God, What Role Do You Play?"

She is a lifter upper of your heads, having endured many hardships as a good soldier. She is the mother of four sons, and the grandmother of 5. She loves to sing and has a heart for people.

My favorite song "I Get Joy When I Think About What He's Done For Me" keeps me in a place of humbleness before God for I have lived to see God turn my mess into an awesome message! Had it not been for Him on my side, I don't know where I would be. I live by the word that says "But the God of all grace, who hath called us unto his eternal glory by Christ Jesus, after that ye have suffered a while, make you perfect, stablish, strengthen, settle you.
I'm Settled. To God Be The Glory.

Bibliography

(1) Piper, J. (2012). The Sovereignty of God. Retrieved from www.desiringgod.org

(2) Oppong, T. (2017). Start Doing These Things for Yourself to Transform Your Life in Less Than a Year. Retrieved from https://medium.com

(3) Corrections, Dept. of (2014). The Strategy Tree. Retrieved from https://vadoc.virginia.gov

(4) Lamele, M. (2015). This Is The Single Greatest Barrier To Discovering Your Life's True Purpose. Retrieved from www.mindbodygreen.com

www.ingramcontent.com/pod-product-compliance
Lightning Source LLC
Chambersburg PA
CBHW042051290426
44110CB00001B/18